Teacher Teac
Making praye

GW00993702

by Winifred Acred FMA

Cover design and photo courtesy of
Saint Brendan's Primary School, Harwood, Bolton.

DON BOSCO

ISBN 0-9538991-5-2
© **Don Bosco Publications**
Thornleigh House Sharples Park Bolton BL1 6PQ Tel 01204 308811
Fax 01204 306868 Email: joan@salesians.org.uk

CONTENTS

To the little people I have taught
who in their turn taught me to pray

INTRODUCTION

Jesus said,

I have come that you may have life

To pray with the young is to give birth to this life or at least to be part of the process. There are all sorts of definitions for prayer. To me it is an occasion for getting in touch with the infinite within us and around us. With this in mind, prayer time in the classroom can be a sacred moment, a bonding time. Teachers with children. Children with children. More importantly a bonding time with a loving Father. Children have a natural gift when it comes to contemplation, but so often we do not help them to develop this gift. Teachers have heavy workloads and prayer can become just an extra task in a very busy day. This book aims at helping to ease some of this pressure and make worship in the classroom a special moment for everyone. An opportunity to give life and strength to all other moments of the day.

Timing is important if teacher and children are going to enjoy a special moment together. While praying first thing in the morning can set the atmosphere for the day it can also be a moment of stress for some children who may come rushing in late and worried. When choosing the time for prayer each teacher should be sensitive to the needs of the class, and her own needs.

Atmosphere is another important factor. The children should be comfortable, preferably sitting on a carpet. If you are not fortunate enough to have a carpeted area why not use 'prayer mats', carpet samples from the local carpet shop. Children love to have their own 'prayer mat'. Mood music, as the children gather, can help set the mood for the prayer session. This does not always have to be classical music. Music from other countries such as African drum music can often set an atmosphere for praise. Pan Pipes can have a very calming effect on the children.

Language and silence, gesture and stillness, are all important when praying with the young. Just as children understand that there is such a thing as 'book language', very soon they understand that there is such a thing as 'prayer language'. However this should not be a stilted way of talking to God their loving Father. They should be encouraged to use their own language while enjoying scripture language. Children can also touch the infinite within short silences provided they are prepared for it by stillness. Imaginary hugs and sending our love to people can be done during silence. Use of the imagination is vital for prayer. Gestures such as hand movements, bowing, blessing etc can help the restless children. It can also add meaning to words.

It may help to have a small prayer corner in the classroom with a candle, a well-chosen picture or icon which is changed according to need or the time of the year. This corner can also be used as a 'thinking corner' where a child might go to calm down after a quarrel or to consider a socially unacceptable action.

A resource box is essential. It could contain materials of different colours and texture, different candles, small prayer cards, a teddy, a beanbag toy, shells, tapes, a memory bowl in which to drop our happy and sad memories, or a memory book.

The appendix to this book deals with situations. What do you do when a child comes into school saying "My granny died last night"? Is it enough to say, "Oh dear, we will pray for her." Hopefully this book will give some ideas, which will help make these important moments special.

Winifred Acred

HOW TO USE THIS BOOK

The sessions in this book are primarily for classroom use, however they can be adapted for general school assembly. They can be dipped into according to need rather than being used in any particular order. Each theme has a story which may be an adaptation of scripture or a parable. These can be read on the first day followed by suggestions for use in prayer. One particular line will be the catch phrase for the week. It will be the thread which links prayer with the events of the day and inspires the children. It may be a phrase from the story or a line from a psalm or hymn. These are only suggestions. Sometimes the children might prefer to choose their own. You yourself may find one more appropriate to the children's needs at the time.

Suggestions for using the catch phrase

It could be printed and put in the prayer corner.
Children might like to write it and decorate their page.
Children could make a bookmark with the prayer.
It could be said as the end of day prayer,
or before going out to play.
It may be appropriate to whisper it to a particular child after some incident.

I AM IMPORTANT

Resource: Tape, *'Together We Can'* by Carey Landry
from North American Liturgy Resources.

Catch Phrase: Together we can do great things

In a little street, not very far from here, there was a house in
which lived a very happy family. Every morning mum or dad
would come down, put on the light then would switch on the
kettle to make the tea. The children would come down to be
greeted by the smell of toast from the toaster. They all loved
their breakfast. Dad and mum would listen to the news on the
radio while the children ate their sugar puffs and toast.

When the children had gone to school dad would quickly
vacuum the carpets and then go off to work. Mum would put
the washing in the washing machine, before she too had to
hurry out to work.

When the door was closed magic things began to happen.
The washing machine said, "Goodness me what a lot of
washing I have to do today." "You should worry," said the
vacuum cleaner, "I had all the downstairs to clean this morning
and the dog leaves so many hairs about. They get down my
pipe and cause me no end of trouble." "Well," said the kettle,
'Make the tea! make the coffee', is all I hear. I don't even get
time to get cold. There is no rest for a poor old kettle." "Hmm,"
sighed the toaster. "One wants it just a little bit brown, another
wants it nearly burnt. I can't keep up with them. I get all hot
and bothered and then I burn everything. I have a horrible
feeling they will throw me out soon." "Oh no!" they all agreed
"you make lovely toast." "What about me," said the little radio,
"did you hear me crackling this morning? I have heard that
there is a new thing called digital something or other, so that
might be the end of me."

Everyone shuddered. The telly smiled and said, "I'm OK. They would sit and look at me all night. Sometimes I wish they would give me a bit of peace and listen to you, Radio."

Saturday morning came and the whole family went shopping. They came back with a very large box. The children were so excited. Dad opened the box very carefully and pulled out what looked like another telly. "Goodness me what's this?" thought the telly. Everyone watched as dad pulled out wires and plugs. "There!" he said, "Look at our new computer." The children cheered and started to fight about who would be first to use it. The family never moved from the computer all day, even past the children's bedtime. Mum and Dad stayed up later playing on the computer. They were so tired they didn't even make a cup of tea.

When everyone was tucked up in bed the computer spoke to all the other electrical things in the house. "Ahmm," he coughed, and then speaking in a very posh voice he said, "Good evening everyone, as you see I have come to live here and I am very important. I expect you to treat me with respect. You may have noticed that last night the family took no notice of any of you and this is the way it is going to be. I have taken over now." There was a general groan from everyone. "What will happen to us?" cried the vacuum cleaner. All the gadgets began to talk at once. The computer sat back with a big smirk on his face feeling very important.

"Wait a minute," said the Telly. "I have an idea." All the gadgets gathered around in a huddle so that the computer couldn't hear. All he could hear were whispers and, "What a good idea, Telly." He felt a bit left out. He wondered what they were planning. Well he didn't care; when the family came home they would soon see who was special.

9

That night, when all the family came home, they again sat around the computer, taking turns and helping each other. The computer felt so proud of himself.

Next morning came the shock. Mum switched on the light but it didn't work. She filled the kettle but it wouldn't boil. "Strange!" said Dad. "The toast isn't brown, it isn't even hot." The radio just crackled, so no one could listen. Everyone was in a bad mood. Dad started arguing with mum, and shouting at the children, who were fighting with each other. It was such a sad house. Dad went off to work slamming the door. Mum said she would get the electrician, but he couldn't come till tomorrow.

When all the family had gone, the computer looked around at all the sad faces. He realised that everyone was special in different ways. Without the light no one could see, without the kettle there was no tea. He realised it was important for them to hear the news, and to have nice toast for breakfast, and that they needed the vacuum cleaner and washing machine to help them do their work. "I'm sorry," said the computer, "I see now how we are all important. I can't do what you do and you can't do what I do. But each one is important to the family. Please forgive me I would like to be your friend." The little toaster wiggled his wires and the washing machine gave a big gurgle of delight. "That's OK," said the telly. "It's good that you understand that in this house everyone is important, and everyone is needed. We all have a special job to do, which no one else can do. That is why we live happily together."

Prayer moment

Let us just close our eyes and think about the story. (*Pause*) Think about all the people in your family, each person is special. (*Pause)* When you have given this some thought just say to yourself, **'Together we can do great things.'**

10

I AM IMPORTANT

DAY 2

Recall the story

Together we can do great things

Quiet moment

Everyone was happy in the house before the computer came.
Each one had their special job.
Could the radio make the toast?
Could the toaster clean the floor?
Could the kettle do the washing?
Could the washing machine make the tea?
It all sounds silly,
but sometimes we think we can do everything.
Whatever I am asked to do I can only do MY BEST.
When I do my best I feel happy.
My best might not be like someone else's,
but it is MY BEST, and with all the others it will make one great big BEST.
Shall we all try to do our PERSONAL BEST today?

Prayer moment

Just open your hands
and raise them up,
say this after me,

"God my Father, I give you my best today."

Let's go now
and be the best people we can be today.

I AM IMPORTANT

DAY 3

Recall the story

Together we can do great things

Quiet moment

Do you remember how mum and dad felt when none of the things in the house worked?

Poor dad he couldn't have his toast, and mum couldn't clean the house or have her cup of tea.

The children weren't very happy either were they?

What would happen if your arm or your hand thought, "I'm not going to do anything today?"

Supposing your legs refused to move?

We need every part of our body just as we need each other. Look around our class.

Supposing there were no other children and we had no friends.

Prayer moment

Close your eyes and make yourself very still. *(Pause)*

Make a picture in your mind of someone in our class whom you don't have much to do with. Perhaps you don't like them very much. *(Pause)*

Try to think of something nice about them. *(Pause)*

In your mind give them a hug. *(Pause)*

Let us thank God that they are in our class. *(Pause)*

How can you work with them today? *(Pause)*

Let us go now

and try to be kind to everyone today so that,

Together we can do great things

I AM IMPORTANT

Recall the story

Together we can do great things

Quiet moment

When all the things worked together how did the family feel?
If we worked together to be our best how would we feel?

Prayer moment

Class stand in a circle holding hands.
Move around slowly chanting rap style
'Together we can do great things'
Start in a whisper,
Slowly getting louder,

going down to a whisper again

or *sing the song, 'Together We Can'.*

I AM LOVED

Resource: *A large mirror and/or a number of small mirrors.*
Hymn: *'If I were a Butterfly'.*

Catch Phrase: Thank you God for making me ME

Coco

Long, long ago there lived an old toy maker. He made lots of toys and he loved them all. He was always happy when boys or girls came to his tiny shop to buy one of his toys.

One day he thought to himself I think I'll make a little puppet. He took a fine piece of wood and started to chip away at it. Chip, chip, chip he went all day, till he had made a fine looking puppet.

He painted the cutest little face and gave him shiny yellow hair. He dressed him in velvet trousers and a blue check shirt. Finally he put strings on his head, and on his hands and feet so that he could run and dance. It was very late when he had finished. The sun had gone down and the bright moon was shining. The old toy maker stood back and looked at his puppet. He thought, "My! What a wonderful little puppet. I don't think I will sell you I'd like to keep you. You are a fine little chap. I think I will call you Coco." He put him high upon a shelf to let his paint dry. The old toy maker smiled to himself as he went up to bed. What a good day I have had making my little puppet, he thought. Soon the old man was fast asleep.

As the clock struck midnight, all the toys began to wake up. Coco looked around rather shyly and said, "Hello!" He saw the pretty doll, and his little wooden heart began to beat faster. Pretty doll looked at him and laughed, "Why have you got such a big wooden nose?"

Coco didn't know what to say. Just then a large teddy bear growled from the corner. "Welcome to the toy shelf," he said in a deep teddy bear kind of voice. "You are a funny creature you haven't got any fur on you." Coco looked at himself and noticed he only had shiny paint and the clothes the toy maker had given him. Left right, left right, quick march, along came a very smart toy soldier. "Good evening," he said to Coco, "Stand up straight." he shouted. "I can't," said Coco, "Someone has to pull my strings." "What!" said the soldier, "You don't have a key or a battery?" "No," sighed Coco, feeling very down. The other toys laughed. The pretty doll giggled and said, "Fancy! He hasn't got a key or a battery. What a funny creature."

Coco did so want all the toys to love him. "I would love to be like the smart toy soldier, or as cuddly as big bear, then maybe pretty doll would like me." He thought for a moment, then before anyone could say a word, he had pulled off his wooden nose, and began to scratch all his lovely shiny paint to see if there was any fur underneath. Finally he found some scissors and cut each of his strings. Snip, snip went the scissors on the strings of his feet. Snip, snip went the scissors on the strings on his head, lastly snip, snip went his hand strings. FLOP, FLOP, FLOP went Coco into a heap on the shelf. The other toys gasped when they saw him, but it was too late; they could hear the toy maker coming down the stairs singing a little tune. They all became very still.

The toy maker came in and made himself a cup of tea, then went over to the shelf to see his new puppet. He couldn't believe his eyes. He picked up the little heap of scratched wood in his arms, and a big tear rolled down his lined cheek, "Oh my poor Coco," he cried. "What have you done?" Coco felt warm, almost alive in the old man's arms. He felt a tear from the old man's brown eyes fall on his little scratched wooden face.

He tried to tell the old man that he only wanted to please the pretty doll, the teddy and the toy soldier. But he felt ashamed. The toy maker held Coco tighter as he whispered, "Oh I loved you just as you were. I made your nose so you could smell the beautiful flowers. I gave you strings so you could run and dance and play with me. I gave you shiny paint and clothes and I thought you looked so handsome." The poor little puppet tried to say 'Sorry' but words wouldn't come. His little wooden heart was beating fast. What will happen now? Would he be thrown away? Would the old man stop loving him? Would all the toys laugh at him?

The old man took the puppet, and smiled saying, "Don't be afraid little fellow, I made you and I love you no matter what you look like or what you do. The way I made you is the way I want you to be." That evening he repainted Coco, added a new piece to his nose, dressed him up again and gave him back his strings. "There you are little one," said the old man. Coco was so happy that his little wooden heart nearly burst with joy. The pretty doll smiled at him and the toy soldier said he would teach him how to march by pulling his strings. The teddy bear growled and gave him a cuddle. Coco knew he was loved, just as he was, and that made him feel good again.

Prayer moment

Close your eyes and just imagine God putting his arms around you and saying,
"I love you." *(Pause)* "I love you just as you are."

Leave the children for a few seconds to absorb these words.

I AM LOVED

DAY 2

Recall the story

Thank you God for making me ME

Quiet moment

Coco wanted to be friends with all the toys.
Why did he feel sad when he met each one?
Develop the idea that they laughed at him because he wasn't like them.
Is there anyone you would like to be?
Can you be them?
Wouldn't it be a funny world if everyone looked the same?
If everyone spoke the same, did the same things, etc.
What would the world be like if all the trees were exactly the same and the flowers and the animals?

Prayer moment

Let us sing a song to thank God for making us and loving us just as we are.
Sing 'If I were a Butterfly' *(with actions).*

I AM LOVED

DAY 3

Recall the story

Thank you God for making me ME

Quiet moment

A large mirror and/or a number of small mirrors.

Coco scratched his paint, pulled off his nose,
and cut his strings to try to make himself different.
How did the toy-maker feel when he saw him?
When God made us he was really pleased with what he had done.
He thought each one of us was beautiful.
Sometimes we laugh at the people God has made.
Sometimes we wish we were different.
How would you feel if you made a lovely model or painted a picture and someone came and laughed at it or said it was rubbish?
Each one here is a beautiful person made by God,
and he loves each one just the way we are.

Prayer moment

Play quiet taped music.
Children walk up to the mirror and look at themselves saying,
Thank you God for making me ME.

I AM LOVED

Recall the story

Thank you God for making me ME

Quiet moment

Coco cut his strings and just flopped on the floor.
The old toy-maker told him he had given him the strings
so that he could have life.
When God made us, instead of strings, he gave us a heart.
This is our contact with him because he loves us
and we love him.
He can help us to be good,
to do all the things he wants us to do.
We have to keep in touch with him,
by talking to him and doing what he wants.

Prayer moment

Quietly think of something that you think God might be asking
you to do today.
Think how you will do it.
Ask God to help you.
Let's all sing the chorus of 'If I were a Butterfly'.

CARING AND SHARING

Resource:
A basket on the prayer table with small pieces of paper cut out as fish and loaves. As the children perform little acts of kindness or sharing they can put in a fish or loaf.

Cards with smiling face .☺

Catch Phrase: Gather up the pieces

JAKE

This story is an adaptation of the scripture story taken from Matthew 14. vv 13-21.

Hello my name is Jacob. My friends call me Jake. My mum calls me all sorts of names, which I won't tell you because they are not very nice! She is always shouting at me. I never seem to do the right thing. She says I am never around when she needs me. You see I like to go fishing and wander over the hills and listen to all the villagers gossiping in the market square.

Do you like adventures? I do. I have lots of adventures. The other day I had the best of my whole life. Let me tell you about it. It was very strange and wonderful at the same time. Mum asked me to go for the bread. I had to get five loaves. I knew she wasn't in a hurry so I went by the lake to do a little fishing. I sat for a while with my fishing rod dangling in the blue water. It was all so peaceful. I sat there dreaming of changing the world. Making everyone happy instead of grumpy. I caught two big fish. I was delighted. I thought I had better get home or there would be another shouting match.
As I wandered up the hill I saw a huge crowd. Well of course I couldn't resist a crowd. It might be a fight, or an accident, so I went over to look.

It wasn't a fight or an accident. It was a man talking to the people. Everyone was listening to him. I pushed my way through to the front of the crowd, being small that was fairly easy. He was talking about loving everyone. He even made me feel I could love my little sister who is a real nuisance because she spoils my toys. This man seemed so strong, yet gentle at the same time. He had the kindest face I had ever seen. It felt good to be near him. He talked all afternoon, and the people listened. I wanted to stay there forever. He had some special friends with him who looked a bit worried. I heard one of them ask the man to send the people home because they would be hungry. The man said, "No, no we will have to feed the people. They have been with me all day. I can't just send them away without something to eat. I feel sorry for them, they must be hungry." I heard one of his friends laugh and say that it would be impossible to feed all these people and, even if we had enough money, all the shops were shut. The man just smiled and said to his friends, "Get the people to sit down and we will see what we can do."

His friends came round to see if anyone had any food to share but everyone said no. Should I tell him about my mum's five loaves and the two fish that I had caught? No, he would only laugh at me; my five loaves and two fish wouldn't go very far anyway. Then a neighbour of mine called Andrew came over; he taught me fishing when I was very tiny. He was also a very special friend of this man. He smiled at me, and asked me what I was doing out here so late. I told him I had a little bit of food if he wanted to share it with me. The next thing I knew he took me by my hand, and led me up to this man. "Tell Jesus what you said to me," he said smiling. I shook all over I was so near Jesus. "Please sir," I said in my best voice, "I have five little loaves and two fish. I was going to take them home to my mum but you can have them if you are hungry".

Jesus gave me the most wonderful smile "Thank you Jake. Thank you for your gift I will share it with all these people." Then he took my little loaves and looked up to heaven. Next he took the fish, my fish which I caught, and again he looked up to heaven. Then, to my surprise, he said to his friends, "Go and give these to the people." My eyes nearly popped out of my head. Every one had some bread and fish and no one was hungry. Then his friends went round and gathered up all the crumbs and they filled 12 baskets.

I ran all the way home to tell my mum. I don't think she believed me till she heard all the people in the market talking about it. Andrew, our neighbour, told my mum how kind I had been with my bread and fishes. Mum was really proud of me. I felt good when I went to bed. I thought how I would like to be one of Jesus' special friends when I grow up. I will follow him wherever he goes.

Quiet moment

Remember what Jesus said, "I feel sorry for the people," and "gather up the crumbs." Perhaps this week we could try to look at other people, and see what they need. We could share what we have. If you do that you can put a little fish in the basket. If you tidy up, and keep the place tidy you can put a little loaf in the basket. Maybe at the end of the week, our little fish and loaves will be like a prayer, for all the people who are hungry.

Prayer moment

Children should be sitting on the mat grouped together like the crowd.
Close your eyes. Make yourself very still.
Just imagine you are sitting on the hill listening to Jesus.
See him looking at you, smiling.
Very short pause.

CARING AND SHARING

Recall the story

Gather up the pieces

Quiet moment

Do you remember what Jake was dreaming about when he sat by the lake?
Yes he was dreaming about changing the world.
I wonder what you would do if you could change the world?
Would you make sure that there was no one who was hungry?
No more wars.
Can you do anything about it?
Maybe not, but we can pray,
and ask God to help people who can.
I can change my little world,
where I live, my classroom, my home.

Prayer moment

Get the children to say a spontaneous prayer for the things they want to change e.g. the hungry, those affected by floods, war etc.

Quietly think of something you could change in yourself
that would make your world a better place.
You might be more loving, more ready to share,
more truthful etc.
Ask Jesus to help you.

CARING AND SHARING

DAY 3

Put the smiley face cards around the room or give each child one for the desk as reminders to smile during the day even if they don't feel like it.

Recall the story

Gather up the pieces

Quiet moment

Remember how Jesus felt sorry for the people
because he thought they might be hungry.
Did he have a lot of food to give them?
Where did he get the food for them?
Did Jake give him enough food for the 5000 people?
Jake only gave a very small thing,
and Jesus used it to make so many people happy.
What small thing could we give today to make others happy?
Jesus can use all the little things we do to make people happy.
Little things mean so much.
When you smile it makes you feel happy.
Your smile can make someone else smile,
and so feel happy too.

Prayer moment

Ask the children to put a big smile on their face and lift up their hands and repeat the prayer after you.
Jesus I will try to smile today.
Please use my smile to make someone happy.

CARING AND SHARING

DAY 4

Recall the story

Gather up the pieces

Quiet moment

Who remembers what Jesus did at the end of the story?
Jesus didn't want to leave any rubbish around.
He wanted to leave our world beautiful,
because that is how his Father made it.
Sometimes we don't like tidying up.
We leave things in a mess for other people.
Do you think that is a kind thing to do?

Prayer moment

This little prayer is chanted.
The first time it should be whispered.
It can be repeated becoming louder but the last one should
be whispered.
Simple tapping or a non-tuned instrument could be used to
give a rhythm.
Teacher: Gather up the pieces
Children: Let's gather up the pieces
Teacher: Make my world beautiful
Children: Let's make our world beautiful.
Repeat the whole chant,
getting louder,
then softer.

OUR WORLD IS HOLY

Resources: *Candles. Incense or perfumed oil and burner.*
Hymn: *'Holy Ground'.*

Catch Phrase: This is Holy Ground

Moses

From Exodus 1-3.

A long time ago God's people lived in a country called Egypt. They were very happy there, till one day a new king called Pharaoh came to rule the land. He did not know how good God's people were. He was a rich and mighty king with a large army. All the people feared him.

Pharaoh noticed that there were many of God's people. He thought that because they were so many they would rise up and take his throne from him. He was scared so he made them into slaves. He made them work hard without any pay. He took away their tools to make their work harder, then he would get his soldiers to beat them. They had to build without anything to make the bricks and work in the fields without anything with which to dig. He did not like the way God's people wanted to worship God. He said they had to worship him because he was the greatest. God's people were very sad. They prayed to God to help them escape from Pharaoh but many years passed and it seemed as though God wasn't listening to their prayers. However God loved his people and he saw how miserable they were and decided it was time to help them.

One day one of God's very special friends called Moses was out minding some sheep. It was a very hot day and he was looking for somewhere to shelter. In the distance he saw a bush. "Hmm," he thought, "I'll go over there and sit down in its shade."

So Moses went nearer to the bush when suddenly he saw something very strange; the bush was on fire but it wasn't getting burnt up. "That's odd," he thought. "I'll go a little closer to see what is really happening." As Moses came near to the burning bush he heard a voice calling him. He looked around but saw no one. Then he heard the voice again "Moses, Moses take off your shoes. You are standing on holy ground." Moses was frightened at first but he bent down and slowly took off his shoes. He felt a strange and sacred presence so he bowed low, right down to the ground. Moses realised that the presence of God was all around him. God spoke to Moses. Moses listened. God said to Moses, "Go and take my people away from Pharaoh so that they can worship me."

Moses was afraid. He bowed low again and said, "Please Lord God, ask someone else. I am not able to talk to Pharaoh." God saw how Moses was worried and said gently, "Don't worry because I am God who has always been and always will be. I will be with you, and your brother Aaron will help you." Moses loved his brother Aaron and he knew he would help him. He bowed low again and trusting in the Lord God said he would do what God wanted. With the Lord God's help he would face the great Pharaoh and set God's people free. But how he did it is another story.

Prayer moment

Close your eyes. (*Pause*)
In your mind think about what you know about God, who loves you.
The most important thing is that he loves me.
(*Allow the children a moment to think about this*)
Amen.

OUR WORLD IS HOLY

DAY 2

Light the candle or the incense well before the prayer session to allow the perfume to penetrate.

Recall the story

This is Holy Ground

Quiet moment

God spoke to Moses and told him to take off his shoes because he was on holy ground. It was holy because God was near. God is near us now. We can always remember that God is near. Our classroom is holy. Let us do what Moses did and bow down before God our Father.

Prayer moment

You may want to allow the children to take off their shoes but this is not essential.
Allow the children to walk all around the room singing softly 'Holy Ground'. Keep singing to allow the children to cover the whole floor space.

OUR WORLD IS HOLY

DAY 3

Light the candle or the incense well before the prayer session to allow the perfume to penetrate.

Recall the story

This is Holy Ground

Quiet moment

When we pray there are different ways of praying.
We can stand or kneel or join our hands or just sit.
When Moses heard God's voice he bowed down to the ground to worship him.
Today let us pray like Moses.

Prayer moment

Get the children to stand up with their hands raised, then slowly kneel and bow down to the ground with their foreheads touching the ground.
When all the children are bowed down say slowly
Lord God you are great, we bow before you.
Or
Lord God you are wonderful, we bow before you.

OUR WORLD IS HOLY

DAY 4

Light the candle or the incense well before the prayer session to allow the perfume to penetrate.

Recall the story

This is Holy Ground

Quiet moment

Moses listened to God then he had to do something for him. He had to take the people away to help them to worship God. God wants us to help people to worship him, to pray to him. We can help each other by praying ourselves the best we can.

Today we will try again to be like Moses **looking** for God, bowing down **worshipping** God, and then **listening** to God.

Prayer moment

Walk around singing 'Holy Ground'.
Stop and bow down worshipping God.
Stay bowed down to quietly listen to God.
Slowly rise singing a praising hymn or 'Holy Ground'.

HAPPINESS IS..

Resources: Small cards with **HAPPINESS IS** printed on with a space to fill in what happiness is.

Catch phrase: Happiness is being loved by God

A CAT CALLED TIGER

One cold wintry night a large black cat lay huddled behind an old building. She was trying to keep her three little kittens warm, as the bitter wind howled through the opening in the wall. The kittens were three weeks old, and she was very proud of them. One was like her, shiny black. The second had little white paws and a white spot on his head. The third was quite different. He looked so ordinary, with brown and black stripes all over his body.

When morning came the little stripped kitten was restless. He began to wander off to explore. He had not gone long when there was a loud frightening noise. He ran as fast as his little paws would take him and hid in a corner. His little body went stiff as he watched a huge machine coming on to the ground knocking down everything in front of it. He heard a man shout, "Stop! Stop!" He saw the man pick up his two little brothers and put them in a box. Then his mum was gently placed in the box and carried off.

"Meow" cried the little kitten, but the big machine was making so much noise knocking down the old house, that no one heard him. Little Kitten hid in the corner all day, frightened of the big machine. When evening came all went quiet. Little Kitten thought he would come out of his hiding place and see if he could find something to eat. As he crept across the rubble of the old house some big boys saw him and started to throw stones at him. Little Kitten was really frightened and hid behind some bricks.

As darkness fell, the lights in the windows twinkled. Little Kitten saw a large white cat slinking along the road. "Meow, Good evening" said Little Kitten. "Meow" said the large white cat in a very posh voice. "I don't talk to stray cats like you. I am a pet cat and my owner looks after me." She walked on with her nose in the air. She walked up the path, scratched the door once, and it was opened. Little Kitten heard a lady's voice welcoming her. He watched enviously as a gentle hand stroked her. "Oh," thought Little Kitten, "I wish I had someone to look after me." As Little Kitten turned away he heard a strange noise "Woof! Woof!" a large ferocious dog came running towards him. Little Kitten ran for his life right up a tree. The dog snarled, and barked and barked as the kitten balanced dangerously on a branch. Soon the dog got tired and strolled off. Little Kitten was trembling with fear. If only he had a home like big white cat. But it was no good just wishing.

Little Kitten found a dustbin and leapt up to see if there was anything for his tea. He managed to scrape out some bits of fish to stop his tummy from rumbling. Poor Little Kitten was now very cold and tired. He curled up in a corner and tried to sleep. Night came. The moon cast strange shadows along the street. He was scared. Oh how he longed to see his mum and little brothers. Pitter-patter down came the rain. Soon Little Kitten was soaking wet. He thought that if he walked along the road he might not feel so cold. He passed many houses, and thought of all the people inside sleeping peacefully.

He thought that there might even be lucky cats sleeping in cosy baskets inside these very houses, and he wished he were one of them. "If I could live in a house I would be the best pet cat ever. I would do just what I was told. I wouldn't give any bother. I wouldn't scratch or make a noise. I would drink all my milk. I would, I would, oh what's the use of thinking what I would do. I will never be anyone's pet. I will just die out here." He lay down under a tree and tried to sleep.

Morning came and Little Kitten woke as the milkman plonked three bottles on the step.Little Kitten went over to the white shiny bottles. He was just putting his tiny paw on the top when a lady came out to take the milk in. "Shoo," she shouted and Little Kitten ran down the path. He heard the door bang and he crept back up the path. He climbed stealthily up onto the dustbin and peered through the kitchen window. Inside he could see a girl eating her breakfast. She glanced round and saw Little Kitten. "Mummy," she cried there is a tiger at the window." Little Kitten jumped off the bin and hid. Mummy came out with the little girl. "Look," said Mummy, "Don't be afraid. It's not a tiger, it's just a little stray kitten." The girl came over to Little Kitten who was crouching behind the bin. She picked him up and stroked him gently. It sent a shiver right down his back. This must be what happiness is thought Little Kitten. The girl carried him gently into the kitchen, fed him on creamy milk and stroked him gently. "Can I keep him Mummy?" she said. Her mum said she could provided no one claimed him. Little Kitten knew that no one else wanted him. This was to be his home, where he would be loved like the big white cat. He felt so happy. "Happiness must be being loved and stroked," thought Little Kitten as he purred away in the girl's arms.

"Mummy," she said "I am going to call my kitten Tiger, because he looks like a tiger the king of the jungle." "Happiness is having a real name," thought kitten. "It makes me feel special."

Prayer moment

Make a picture in your mind of Tiger being stroked.
Just think how he felt.
Think of yourself being cuddled by someone you love.
Feel how much they love you.
Wrap your arms around yourself and say together,
Happiness is being cuddled by some one. *Repeat slowly.*

HAPPINESS IS..

DAY 2

Recall the story

Happiness is being loved by God

Quiet moment

Remember how Little Kitten felt all alone in the rain.

He was hungry.

He was frightened.

He had no friends.

Prayer moment

Stand in a space in the room not near anyone else.

Close your eyes. Think of all the lonely people in the world.

In your mind put your arms around them so they can feel your love.

Ask Jesus to take your love to them.

Say together,

Happiness is having someone to care for you.

HAPPINESS IS..

DAY 3

*Prepare small pieces of card with the words, **happiness for me is...***

Recall the story

Happiness is being loved by God

Quiet moment

Little Kitten saw the white cat being stroked and thought that must be happiness.

He saw the lights in the houses twinkling and wanted to be inside. Was that happiness for him?

What makes you happy? Really happy?

Prayer moment

Sometime during the day write (or draw) on your card what happiness is for you.

When you have written it, place your card on the prayer table. Ask your loving Father to give you that happiness.

HAPPINESS IS..

DAY 4

Recall the story

Happiness is being loved by God

Quiet moment

The girl gave Little Kitten a new name.
He felt special because he was called after the king of the jungle even though he was only tiny.
He was special to this little girl.

Prayer moment

God calls us by our name.
We belong to him.
He loves us.
No matter what happens he still loves us.
Let's say together,
Happiness is being loved by God.
(Repeat softly getting louder and ending with a whisper)

SAYING 'YES'

Resources: *An icon of Mary with the word YES printed in large decorative letters.*

Catch Phrase: Saying 'Yes' to God

A SURPRISE VISITOR

Part of the following story is an adapatation of Luke 1 vv 26-38

I am an ordinary young girl, I lived in a little village called Nazareth where nothing much ever happened. We lived a quiet life with everyone in the village knowing everyone else. Strangers very rarely came to the village. The women used to meet at the well when we went for water. Here we would share news and chat about family matters. The only exciting thing that ever happened was one hot day when Rachel's donkey tried to get a drink at the well and got his head stuck in the bucket. His braying could be heard all around the village as he kicked and bucked trying to get his head out of the bucket. The men folk came running in from the fields to see what was happening. It was such a funny sight everyone was laughing. When Rachel's dad Jacob finally pulled the bucket off his head the donkey ran off into the field with Rachel running after it.

That was just a funny experience. Let me now tell you about something wonderful that happened to me one day. I had been grinding the corn with my mother. She had just gone out to feed the chickens. I began to sweep the floor. I remember I was humming a little tune to myself because I was happy. I was going to marry Joseph the local carpenter. Suddenly I had a strange feeling that there was someone else in the room. I didn't hear anyone I just felt a presence.

I turned round and, believe it or not, I saw an angel standing in front of me. I had never seen an angel before so I was really scared especially when he said I should be happy because I was special. He told me that God was pleased with me so I shouldn't be afraid. He actually said, "Don't be afraid Mary." Yes, he used my name Mary. He said he had a special message from God who wanted to send his Son to our world. He could only do this if he had someone who would be his mother. He asked me if I would be his mother. Me! To be the mother of God's son! I was only good enough to be his servant. I was deeply shocked and very scared. All sorts of things were going through my head. I found it hard to take in what he was saying. I remember asking the angel a lot of questions as to how this could happen.

The angel was very kind and answered all my questions. I had read my bible so I knew that the mother of the saviour would have a very hard time even though he would be a prince. I knew that lots of people would hate him and he would suffer. What should I do? Nothing seemed to make sense at that moment. Deep down in my heart I knew there was only one thing I could do if God asked me to do something. That was to say YES. But maybe I was dreaming or just imagining this angel yet somehow I knew it wasn't a dream. I had a great feeling of happiness in his presence even though I felt afraid at first. With great trust in God I bowed my head and said I would do anything my God asked me. Such joy filled my heart at that moment I can't begin to tell you how happy I felt. I have never stopped singing his praises.

So many things happened to me after that because I said Yes to God. Some were happy, some were sad and hard. Once my baby was born I knew nothing else mattered except doing what he wanted.

Prayer moment

Mary was doing ordinary things while God her loving Father was watching her and smiling upon her.

Close your eyes. (*Pause*)
Make yourself very still. (*Pause*)
Just feel God near you, loving you. (*Pause*)

SAYING 'YES'

DAY 2

Recall the story

Saying 'Yes' to God

Quiet moment

The angel told Mary not to be afraid.
Sometimes we are afraid.
Just think of something you are afraid of.

Prayer moment

In your mind put the thing you are afraid of in a big box.
(Pause) It won't hurt you. Tie it up. *(Pause)* Now imagine
God is holding out his hands to take the box away from you.
He says, "Don't be afraid, I am pleased with you." Today and
tonight we will leave our fears with God. They have gone
away into God's hands.

SAYING 'YES'

DAY 3

Recall the story

Saying 'Yes' to God

Quiet moment

The angel asked Mary to do something very special for God.
Every day God asks us to do little things.
We don't see an angel, but we do hear other people asking us to do something.
Sometimes it's our mum or dad; sometimes it's a friend.
We have to be ready to help everyone.
That means we are helping God to make a better world.

Prayer moment

Sit very still and open your hands turning your palms up to God to show that you are ready to work for him.
While I say the prayer I want you to be like the music whispering 'Yes!' 'Yes!' 'Yes!' over and over.
The teacher then prays the prayer while the children keep whispering chant style 'Yes'
It *might be helpful if the teacher starts the chant with the children so that they get the rhythm.*
Teacher: "Lord God how great you are."
            "I want to do your will." *(Repeat)*

SAYING 'YES'

DAY 4

Recall the story

Saying 'Yes' to God

Quiet moment

Mary said yes to the angel and this meant that Jesus could come and live with us, and show us the way to heaven.

For hundreds of years people have been saying a special prayer to remember Mary saying YES.

They used to say it three times a day, morning noon and evening. Often the church bell would ring at that time to show how happy people were because Mary had said YES to God and Jesus had come to live with us.

We could learn that prayer too

Prayer moment

Children's Angelus
The angel Gabriel came to Mary,
To ask her to be God's mother.

Mary said yes to the angel,
And Jesus was born in a stable.

Thank you for saying yes to God, Mary.
Help me to say yes to God too.

Amen.

FRIENDS

Resources: quiet reflective music.

Catch Phrase: I am coming to your house

Zacchaeus

The following story is an adaptation of Luke 19. vv 1-10

I am a very happy man today but I haven't always been happy. Let me tell you about it. My name is Zacchaeus. I was not always a very nice person. I have changed and that is what I want to tell you about.

I was employed by the Roman soldiers to collect the people's taxes. No one likes paying taxes especially to the Romans who had conquered our town, I was also a little bit greedy. I used to charge the people more than I should and take the extra money for myself. I had become quite rich, yet I was quite lonely because no one wanted to be friends with me.

It was a holiday and I had just come out of my house, to go for a walk, when I saw a large crowd coming down my street. I couldn't see what it was all about, because I am very small. A young boy near me told me that the great teacher and healer was coming. I couldn't believe my luck. I had heard about this man, his name was Jesus. I had heard that he had a friend called Matthew, who had also been a tax collector like me. Maybe Jesus would be my friend. Oh how I would love to have a friend.

I tried looking over the heads of the people but I couldn't see a thing. Then I spied a tree nearby, and before you could say 'Jack Robinson', I had climbed up into it's sturdy branches. I had a wonderful view. I could see Jesus coming down the street. He was smiling and talking.

Every so often he would stop and put his hands on a sick person and they would jump up and praise God. What a man! I had never seen anyone quite like him and yet, at the same time, he looked so ordinary.

I got quite excited as he came near my tree. Suddenly my whole world changed. I was hanging on to the branches and he was looking up at me. The people were laughing, I think they thought I would fall. Then, all of a sudden, a silence descended on the crowd. I could hear Jesus speaking to me saying, "Come down Zacchaeus, I want to come to your house for tea." I couldn't believe my ears. I almost fell off the last branch, as I scrambled down to face Jesus. I could hear some people in the crowd saying, "Fancy Jesus going to his house. He is a tax collector." Jesus didn't seem to mind. I took him to my house. Can you believe it, Jesus in my house! I still can't believe it happened to me, but it did.

He looked so loving and kind that I wanted to be like him. While we were having tea, I promised him that I wouldn't be mean or greedy anymore and that I would give back what I owed people. In fact I would give them three times more than I owed them. We had a wonderful time together. We became great friends and I have tried to be good ever since. Now I have lots of friends.

Prayer moment

Zacchaeus was a funny little man wasn't he? Can you imagine him up that tree trying to see Jesus?
Close your eyes.
Make yourself very still.
Now in your mind pretend to climb the tree *(Pause)*.
Now look down and see only Jesus.
Just watch Jesus talking to people.
Leave the children for a short while to their own imagination.

FRIENDS

Recall the story

I am coming to your house

Quiet moment

Let's think why Zacchaeus had no friends.
He used to be greedy and take all the extra money.
Are we greedy, sometimes?
Do we share our things?

Prayer moment

Close your eyes and immagine Jesus is looking at you.
He is asking you to share something today.
In your heart tell him what you will try to share. *(Pause)*
Let's begin by sharing our love.

Children hold hands and sing

'Let there be love shared among us.'

or

'Love is something you can give away.'

FRIENDS

DAY 3

Recall the story

I am coming to your house

Quiet moment

Jesus asked Zacchaeus if he could come to his house.
Zacchaeus was quite excited at the thought of Jesus in his
house. Jesus will come to us if we want.
All we have to do is close our eyes and ask him.

Prayer moment

Play some soft quiet music.
Say the following slowly pausing at the end of each line.
Let's close our eyes.
Make yourselves very still, imagine you meet Jesus.
He asks you if he can come to your 'house'.
You might feel quite excited.
It means that Jesus is coming to YOU.
You may want to sit down with him, talk to him.
You may want to tell him anything you like.
Tell him anything that is worrying you.
Tell him how much you love him.
Tell him that you are going to try to be very good.
Don't forget to give him a big hug.
When you are ready open your eyes.

FRIENDS

DAY 4

Recall the story

I am coming to your house

Quiet moment

Zacchaeus wanted a friend. Without friends we can feel very lonely. We are lucky in our class because we can all be friends. Can you imagine coming to school and no one playing with you. Can you imagine having no friends?

Prayer moment

Let's hold hands. Close our eyes and think of our friends. Just thank Jesus for our friends. Now let's go round and either shake hands with everyone, or give a hug, to show we all want to be friends.

Let's pray today to be friends with everyone.

Don't leave anyone out.

PRAYERS FOR OCCASIONS

WHEN A CHILD'S RELATIVE HAS DIED

MY GRAN DIED LAST NIGHT

If the child is not showing outward signs of distress ask her to tell the class something about her grandmother when the children are gathered together. If this would be too distressing just say a few words about how wonderful grandmothers are, or whichever relative has died. Ask all the children to think about their grandmother (or relative) and in their mind give them a hug.

Now let us all give N's grandmother a hug and ask Jesus to take her into his home in heaven.
Now in our mind let's all wrap our love round N (child) and her family.

PRAYERS FOR OCCASIONS

WHEN A CHILD TELLS YOU SOMEONE IS ILL

During prayer time tell the children about the sick person.
Ask the children to close their eyes and imagine a picture of
Jesus

Take Jesus by the hand and ask him to go to N, the sick person.

Ask Jesus to stay with the sick person and make them feel happy.

Now let us send our love to that sick person.

We will leave Jesus with that person.

PRAYERS FOR OCCASIONS

The whole class is in trouble

Having appealed to their team spirit and discussed the incident ask the children what they think they should do.
When all the new resolutions and apologies have been made get the class to join hands in a circle.

Let's say a short prayer,
Dear God we are sorry for what we have done.
(*i.e. bad behaviour at assembly or rough behaviour on the playground etc.*)

Let's sing 'We will try to work together' *(to the tune of 'Here we go round the Mulberry Bush'.)*

> We will try to work together,
> work together, work together.
> We will try to work together,
> and learn to love each other.
>
> We will try to work together,
> work together, work together.
> We will try to work together,
> to please our brother Jesus.

PRAYERS FOR OCCASIONS

There has been a big quarrel or incident in the class

Once the offending groups have had time to think,
and say sorry to each other,
recall the incident at a prayer time.
Remind the children that God loves us no matter what we do
Get the children to join hands.
Let's sing "We will try to work together" *(to the tune of Here we go round the Mulberry Bush).*

> This is the way we all forgive,
> all forgive, all forgive.
> This is the way we all forgive,
> and learn to love each other.
>
> This is the way we show our love,
> show our love, show our love.
> This is the way we show our love,
> and live our life together.